# Skills Builders

# Times Tables

3, 4, 6 AND 8

## Hilary Koll and Steve Mills

RISING ★ STARS

Rising Stars UK Ltd, 7 Hatchers Mews, Bermondsey Street, London SE1 3GS
www.risingstars-uk.com

Every effort has been made to trace copyright holders and obtain their permission for the use of copyright materials. The publishers will gladly receive information enabling them to rectify any error or omission in subsequent editions.

All facts are correct at time of going to press.

Published 2013
Text, design and layout © 2013 Rising Stars UK Ltd

Project manager: Dawn Booth
Editorial: Roanne Charles
Proofreader: Jane Jackson
Design: Words & Pictures Ltd, London
Cover design: Amina Dudhia
Illustrations: David Thompson

British Library Cataloguing-in-Publication Data
A CIP record for this book is available from the British Library.

ISBN: 978-0-85769-687-8
Printed in Singapore by Craft Print International

# Skills Builders: Times Tables

3, 4, 6
AND
8

# Contents

# How to use this book

What we have included:

- Each unit covers aspects of the multiplication and division facts related to the 3, 4, 6 and 8 times tables.

- Each unit provides opportunity to practise recalling the number facts in and out of order. You can time yourself to see how you are progressing.

- We have included questions that involve a range of mathematical vocabulary, such as product, shared between, divided by, multiple and so on.

- There are three sections of word problems to ensure that you can use your times tables and division facts in many different contexts.

- All answers are included so you can check your progress.

**1** Some units begin with a useful tip to help you work out answers to the questions more quickly.

**2** **Test 1** involves answering the facts from the times table, usually presented in order. This helps you to see what the unit is about and what you must memorise.

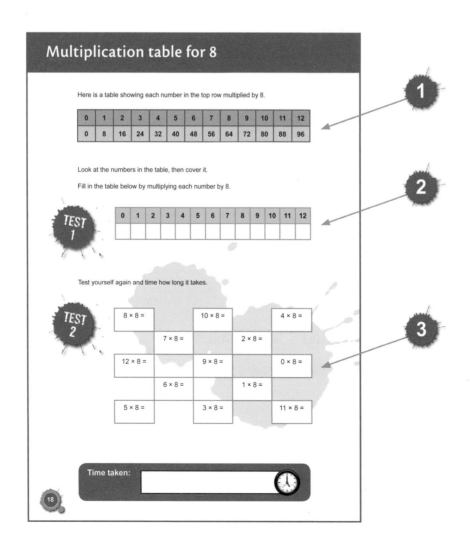

## Multiplication table for 8

Here is a table showing each number in the top row multiplied by 8.

| 0 | 1 | 2 | 3 | 4 | 5 | 6 | 7 | 8 | 9 | 10 | 11 | 12 |
|---|---|---|---|---|---|---|---|---|---|----|----|----|
| 0 | 8 | 16 | 24 | 32 | 40 | 48 | 56 | 64 | 72 | 80 | 88 | 96 |

Look at the numbers in the table, then cover it.

Fill in the table below by multiplying each number by 8.

**TEST 1**

| 0 | 1 | 2 | 3 | 4 | 5 | 6 | 7 | 8 | 9 | 10 | 11 | 12 |
|---|---|---|---|---|---|---|---|---|---|----|----|----|
| | | | | | | | | | | | | |

Test yourself again and time how long it takes.

**TEST 2**

| 8 × 8 = | | 10 × 8 = | | 4 × 8 = |
| | 7 × 8 = | | 2 × 8 = | |
| 12 × 8 = | | 9 × 8 = | | 0 × 8 = |
| | 6 × 8 = | | 1 × 8 = | |
| 5 × 8 = | | 3 × 8 = | | 11 × 8 = |

Time taken:

18

# How to use this book

**3**    **Test 2** gives similar questions but usually in a different order to make sure you learn them in any order. You can also time yourself to see how quickly you can answer them.

**4**    **Warming up** – This section is based on the same number facts as the tests but are presented in words, using mathematical language you should know.

**5**    **Getting hotter** – This section involves word problems. You'll need to use the facts you are learning to answer them. Read them very carefully.

**6**    **Burn it up** – This section has even more challenging questions and problems. You'll need to think very carefully and read each question several times to make sure you reach the correct answer.

**7**    **How did I do?** This gives you a chance to show how confident you feel about the number facts and to say how well you think you are doing.

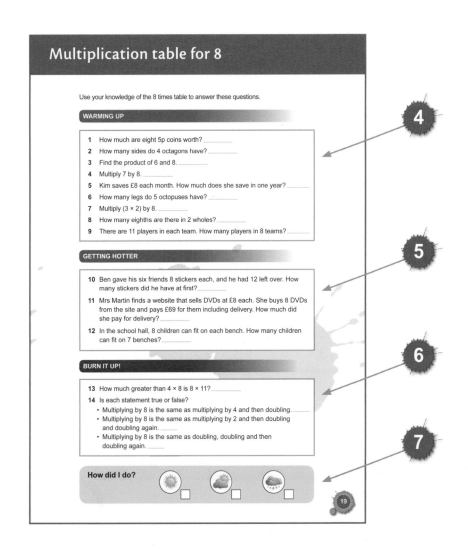

## Multiplication table for 8

Use your knowledge of the 8 times table to answer these questions.

**WARMING UP**

1. How much are eight 5p coins worth? _____
2. How many sides do 4 octagons have? _____
3. Find the product of 6 and 8. _____
4. Multiply 7 by 8. _____
5. Kim saves £8 each month. How much does she save in one year? _____
6. How many legs do 5 octopuses have? _____
7. Multiply (3 × 2) by 8. _____
8. How many eighths are there in 2 wholes? _____
9. There are 11 players in each team. How many players in 8 teams? _____

**GETTING HOTTER**

10. Ben gave his six friends 8 stickers each, and he had 12 left over. How many stickers did he have at first? _____
11. Mrs Martin finds a website that sells DVDs at £8 each. She buys 8 DVDs from the site and pays £69 for them including delivery. How much did she pay for delivery? _____
12. In the school hall, 8 children can fit on each bench. How many children can fit on 7 benches? _____

**BURN IT UP!**

13. How much greater than 4 × 8 is 8 × 11? _____
14. Is each statement true or false?
    - Multiplying by 8 is the same as multiplying by 4 and then doubling. _____
    - Multiplying by 8 is the same as multiplying by 2 and then doubling and doubling again. _____
    - Multiplying by 8 is the same as doubling, doubling and then doubling again. _____

**How did I do?** ☐ ☐ ☐

19

# Multiplication table for 3

Look at the multiples of 3 above the line and the related multiplications below. Then cover them up and test yourself.

| 3 | 6 | 9 | 12 | 15 | 18 | 21 | 24 | 27 | 30 | 33 | 36 |
|---|---|---|----|----|----|----|----|----|----|----|----|

| 1×3 | 2×3 | 3×3 | 4×3 | 5×3 | 6×3 | 7×3 | 8×3 | 9×3 | 10×3 | 11×3 | 12×3 |
| 3×1 | 3×2 | 3×3 | 3×4 | 3×5 | 3×6 | 3×7 | 3×8 | 3×9 | 3×10 | 3×11 | 3×12 |

**TEST 1**

3 × 5 =

3 × 3 =

1 × 3 =

3 × 10 =

3 × 4 =

6 × 3 =

3 × 7 =

8 × 3 =

3 × 9 =

2 × 3 =

11 × 3 =

12 × 3 =

Remember too that zero times any number is zero, so 0 × 3 = 0, and 3 × 0 = 0. Now test yourself again and time yourself.

**TEST 2**

| 3 × 11 = | 8 × 3 = | 3 × 4 = | 7 × 3 = |
|----------|---------|---------|---------|
| 1 × 3 = | 3 × 3 = | 9 × 3 = | 3 × 0 = |
| 3 × 12 = | 10 × 3 = | 0 × 3 = | 3 × 6 = |
| 2 × 3 = | 6 × 3 = | 3 × 9 = | 5 × 3 = |

**Time taken:**

# Multiplication table for 3

Use your knowledge of the 3 times table to answer these questions.

WARMING UP

1   How many sides do 6 triangles have? _____

2   Multiply nine by three. _____

3   What is 12 multiplied by 3? _____

4   What is three times seven? _____

5   Find the product of 3 and 3. _____

6   What are three groups of 11? _____

7   What are four threes? _____

8   Zero times three is what number? _____

9   A cup of coffee costs £3. How much for 8 cups? _____

## GETTING HOTTER

10  A parcel weighs 3 kg. If it costs £2 per kilogram to send the parcel, how much does the parcel cost in total? _____

11  Joe counts on in threes starting at 3. He says the multiples of 3 aloud. What does he say is the 6th multiple of 3? _____

12  Zemar has some football cards that are each 3 cm wide. If he places eight of them touching side by side, how wide is the line of cards? _____

## BURN IT UP!

13  What is the difference between 7 × 3 and 11 × 3? _____

14  An equilateral triangle has sides of 12 cm. What is the perimeter of the triangle? _____

## How did I do?

 ☐     ☐     ☐

# Division facts for 3

Look at the division facts below, cover them up, then test yourself.

| |
|---|
| 0 ÷ 3 = 0 |
| 3 ÷ 3 = 1 |
| 6 ÷ 3 = 2 |
| 9 ÷ 3 = 3 |
| 12 ÷ 3 = 4 |
| 15 ÷ 3 = 5 |
| 18 ÷ 3 = 6 |
| 21 ÷ 3 = 7 |
| 24 ÷ 3 = 8 |
| 27 ÷ 3 = 9 |
| 30 ÷ 3 = 10 |
| 33 ÷ 3 = 11 |
| 36 ÷ 3 = 12 |

**TEST 1**

| |
|---|
| 0 ÷ 3 = |
| 3 ÷ 3 = |
| 6 ÷ 3 = |
| 9 ÷ 3 = |
| 12 ÷ 3 = |
| 15 ÷ 3 = |
| 18 ÷ 3 = |
| 21 ÷ 3 = |
| 24 ÷ 3 = |
| 27 ÷ 3 = |
| 30 ÷ 3 = |
| 33 ÷ 3 = |
| 36 ÷ 3 = |

Tennis balls can be bought in packs of three. Write how many packs have been bought for each basket of balls.

**TEST 2**

| 24 balls | 33 balls | 12 balls | 9 balls | 15 balls |

| 21 balls | 30 balls | 36 balls | 27 balls | 18 balls |

**Time taken:**

# Division facts for 3

Use your knowledge of the division facts for the 3 times table to answer these questions.

WARMING UP

1  How many £3 magazines can you buy with £15? ................

2  What is 6 divided by 3? ................

3  How many threes in 9? ................

4  Divide 12 by 3. ................

5  How many groups of 3 are in 36? ................

6  How many threes in thirty? ................

7  What is zero divided by 3? ................

8  What is the remainder if 28 is divided by 3? ................

GETTING HOTTER

9  How many three-leaved clovers are there if there are 18 leaves altogether? ................

10  A factory makes three-wheeled cars. They have 27 tyres. How many cars can they make? ................

11  A guinea pig is three times longer than a hamster. If the guinea pig is 33 cm long, how long is the hamster? ................

BURN IT UP!

12  A secret number is multiplied by 3. The answer is 7 greater than the answer to 6 ÷ 3. What is the secret number? ................

13  True or false? Dividing an even number by 3 always gives an even answer. ................

14  True or false? Dividing an odd multiple of 3 by 3 always gives an odd answer. ................

**How did I do?**

Multiplying a number by 4 is the same as doubling the number and then doubling the answer, so 3 × 4 is double 3 = 6, then double 6 = 12.

Match the questions and answers with lines

**TEST 1**

| 0 × 4 | double 2 and double again | 8 |
| 1 × 4 | double 1 and double again | 12 |
| 2 × 4 | double 0 and double again | 0 |
| 3 × 4 | double 5 and double again | 16 |
| 4 × 4 | double 4 and double again | 20 |
| 5 × 4 | double 3 and double again | 4 |
| 6 × 4 | double 7 and double again | 44 |
| 7 × 4 | double 6 and double again | 28 |
| 8 × 4 | double 10 and double again | 24 |
| 9 × 4 | double 9 and double again | 48 |
| 10 × 4 | double 8 and double again | 32 |
| 11 × 4 | double 12 and double again | 40 |
| 12 × 4 | double 11 and double again | 36 |

**TEST 2**

Now answer these questions as quickly as you can. Time yourself. Remember, 4 × 6 has the same answer as 6 × 4, and so on.

 0 × 4  4 × 6  4 × 4  4 × 10  7 × 4

 4 × 9  12 × 4  8 × 4  4 × 12  4 × 3  2 × 4

 9 × 4  1 × 4  4 × 0  11 × 4 5 × 4

**Time taken:**

# Multiplication table for 4

Remember that answers to questions on the 4 times table are even numbers.

## WARMING UP

1   How much are four 10p coins worth? _____

2   One-quarter of a number is 2. What is the number? _____

3   How many sides do 6 squares have? _____

4   Multiply 12 by 4. _____

5   Find the product of 4 and 8. _____

6   How heavy are nine 4 kg weights? _____

7   How many legs do 7 sheep have? _____

8   What are eleven lots of four? _____

9   How many legs are there on 12 tables? _____

10  How many wheels on 8 cars? _____

## GETTING HOTTER

11  When Sam was 8 years old he got £4 pocket money each week.
    How much did Sam get in seven weeks? _____

12  There are four football teams in a competition. Each team has 11 players.
    How many players is this altogether? _____

13  Some oranges are cut into quarters. How many quarters are there if
    there were 8 oranges? _____

## BURN IT UP!

14  What is the difference between the number of days in four weeks and
    the number of months in four years? _____

15  Some chairs are arranged into 9 rows. Each row has 4 chairs. 26 people
    sit in the chairs. How many empty seats are there? _____

**How did I do?**    ☐    ☐    ☐

# Division facts for 4

Dividing by 4 is the same as halving and halving again.

Match the questions and answers with lines. One has been done for you.

**TEST 1**

| | | |
|---|---|---|
| 0 ÷ 4 | halve 8 and halve again | 0 |
| 4 ÷ 4 | halve 4 and halve again | 1 |
| 8 ÷ 4 | halve 0 and halve again | 4 |
| 12 ÷ 4 | halve 12 and halve again | 3 |
| 16 ÷ 4 | halve 20 and halve again | 5 |
| 20 ÷ 4 | halve 16 and halve again | 2 |
| 24 ÷ 4 | halve 28 and halve again | 8 |
| 28 ÷ 4 | halve 32 and halve again | 6 |
| 32 ÷ 4 | halve 24 and halve again | 7 |
| 36 ÷ 4 | halve 48 and halve again | 10 |
| 40 ÷ 4 | halve 40 and halve again | 9 |
| 44 ÷ 4 | halve 44 and halve again | 12 |
| 48 ÷ 4 | halve 36 and halve again | 11 |

Now answer these questions as quickly as you can. Time yourself.

**TEST 2**

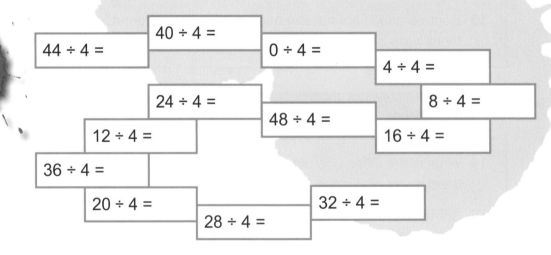

40 ÷ 4 =

44 ÷ 4 =

0 ÷ 4 =

4 ÷ 4 =

24 ÷ 4 =

8 ÷ 4 =

48 ÷ 4 =

12 ÷ 4 =

16 ÷ 4 =

36 ÷ 4 =

20 ÷ 4 =

32 ÷ 4 =

28 ÷ 4 =

**Time taken:**

# Division facts for 4

Can you answer these questions using what you know about dividing by 4?

## WARMING UP

1 How many wholes are 40 quarters? ........................

2 Share 32 grapes between four. ........................

3 Divide 36 by 4. ........................

4 Four times a number is 28. What is the number? ........................

5 How many fours in twenty-four? ........................

6 There are 44 people. They are put into four equal teams.
  How many are in each team? ........................

7 Halve twelve and halve again. ........................

8 How many 4p sweets can you buy with 48p? ........................

## GETTING HOTTER

9 Tickets for a school play cost £4 each. How many tickets can Mrs Lee
  buy for £24? ........................

10 Apples come in packs of 4. How many packs should I buy if I need 16
   apples altogether? ........................

## BURN IT UP!

11 Find the difference between one-quarter of 32 and one-quarter of 16.

   ........................

12 What is the remainder when 50 is divided by 4? ........................

13 A car uses 1 litre of petrol to travel 4 kilometres. How many litres will
   it take to travel 32 kilometres, and how much will this cost if petrol is
   £4 per litre? ........................

## How did I do?

 ☐  ☐  ☐

# Multiplication table for 6

Look at the tables below. Notice that the ×6 answers are double the ×3 answers. Now cover the tables and test yourself.

**TEST 1**

| | | |
|---|---|---|
| 0 × 3 = 0 | 0 × 6 = 0 | 0 × 6 = |
| 1 × 3 = 3 | 1 × 6 = 6 | 1 × 6 = |
| 2 × 3 = 6 | 2 × 6 = 12 | 2 × 6 = |
| 3 × 3 = 9 | 3 × 6 = 18 | 3 × 6 = |
| 4 × 3 = 12 | 4 × 6 = 24 | 4 × 6 = |
| 5 × 3 = 15 | 5 × 6 = 30 | 5 × 6 = |
| 6 × 3 = 18 | 6 × 6 = 36 | 6 × 6 = |
| 7 × 3 = 21 | 7 × 6 = 42 | 7 × 6 = |
| 8 × 3 = 24 | 8 × 6 = 48 | 8 × 6 = |
| 9 × 3 = 27 | 9 × 6 = 54 | 9 × 6 = |
| 10 × 3 = 30 | 10 × 6 = 60 | 10 × 6 = |
| 11 × 3 = 33 | 11 × 6 = 66 | 11 × 6 = |
| 12 × 3 = 36 | 12 × 6 = 72 | 12 × 6 = |

Test yourself again here, and time how long it takes.

**TEST 2**

| 12 × 6 | 2 × 6 | 10 × 6 | 3 × 6 |
|---|---|---|---|

| 9 × 6 | 5 × 6 | 7 × 6 | 4 × 6 | 11 × 6 |
|---|---|---|---|---|

| 8 × 6 | 6 × 6 | 1 × 6 | 0 × 6 |
|---|---|---|---|

**Time taken:**

# Multiplication table for 6

Try these questions about the 6 times table.

## WARMING UP

1. How much are six 5p coins worth? _____
2. How many sides do 4 hexagons have? _____
3. Find the product of 6 and 6. _____
4. How much do eight £6 books cost? _____
5. What do nine 6 g weights weigh? _____
6. Multiply 6 by 11. _____
7. What is six times zero? _____
8. How many eggs are there in 12 boxes of 6? _____
9. Find 10 groups of 6. _____
10. What are six threes? _____

## GETTING HOTTER

11. Mel is saving to buy a computer game costing £45. She has saved £7 each week for 6 weeks. How much more money does she need to buy the game? _____

12. Jiri can jog at a speed of 6 kilometres per hour. How far can he jog in 2 hours at this speed? _____

## BURN IT UP!

13. How much will five chews cost, if six chews cost 48p? _____

14. Find the difference between 6 × 9 and 2 × 6. _____

15. A regular hexagon has sides that are each 6 cm long. How much longer is its perimeter than the perimeter of a square with sides of 6 cm? _____

## How did I do?

 ☐　 ☐　 ☐

# Division facts for 6

Division is the opposite of multiplication. $3 \times 6 = 18$ ⟶ $18 \div 6 = 3$

Write a division question for each multiplication question.

**TEST 1**

$0 \times 6 = 0$ ⟶ $0 \div 6 = 0$         $7 \times 6 =$ ⟶ ..............

$1 \times 6 = 6$ ⟶ $6 \div 6 = 1$         $8 \times 6 =$ ⟶ ..............

$2 \times 6 = 12$ ⟶ $12 \div 6 =$ ......       $9 \times 6 =$ ⟶ ..............

$3 \times 6 = 18$ ⟶ ..............         $10 \times 6 =$ ⟶ ..............

$4 \times 6 = 24$ ⟶ ..............         $11 \times 6 =$ ⟶ ..............

$5 \times 6 = 30$ ⟶ ..............         $12 \times 6 =$ ⟶ ..............

$6 \times 6 =$ ...... ⟶ ..............

Now divide each of these numbers by 6 as quickly as you can. Time yourself.

**TEST 2**

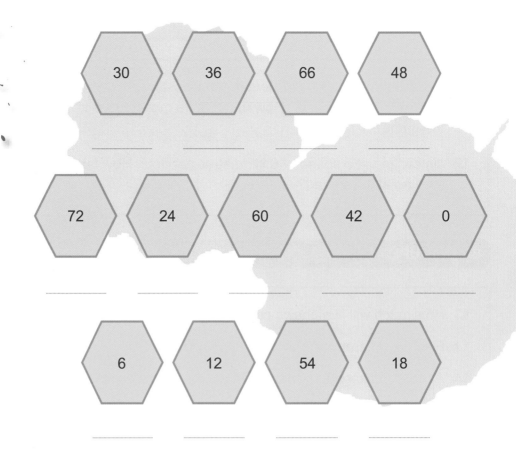

**Time taken:**

# Division facts for 6

Remember your division facts for 6 to help you answer these.

## WARMING UP

1 How many sixes in 36? ..............................

2 66 children are put into 6 teams. How many in each team? ..............................

3 How many boxes of 6 eggs hold 42 eggs? ..............................

4 What is one-sixth of 72? ..............................

5 60 players. How many teams of 6? ..............................

6 Share 54 between 6. ..............................

7 How many 6p sweets can you buy with three 10p coins? ..............................

8 Divide 48 by 6. ..............................

9 What is the remainder when 10 is divided by 6? ..............................

## GETTING HOTTER

10 A wasp flew at a speed of 6 metres per second. How long did it take it to fly 48 metres? ..............................

11 Divide 36 by 6 and then divide the answer by 6. What do you get? ..............................

12 The entrance fee to a funfair is £6. How many tickets can you buy with £66? ..............................

## BURN IT UP!

13 A shop sells T-shirts all at the same price. If five T-shirts cost £20, how much would six T-shirts cost? ..............................

14 A teacher bought some chocolate bars at the end of term. He breaks each bar into 6 chunks and puts them on a plate to hand around. Each child in his class takes 2 chunks, and he eats the last 4 chunks himself. If there are 28 children in his class, how many bars did he buy? ..............................

## How did I do?

# Multiplication table for 8

Here is a table showing each number in the top row multiplied by 8.

| 0 | 1 | 2 | 3 | 4 | 5 | 6 | 7 | 8 | 9 | 10 | 11 | 12 |
|---|---|---|---|---|---|---|---|---|---|----|----|----|
| 0 | 8 | 16 | 24 | 32 | 40 | 48 | 56 | 64 | 72 | 80 | 88 | 96 |

Look at the numbers in the table, then cover it.

Fill in the table below by multiplying each number by 8.

**TEST 1**

| 0 | 1 | 2 | 3 | 4 | 5 | 6 | 7 | 8 | 9 | 10 | 11 | 12 |
|---|---|---|---|---|---|---|---|---|---|----|----|----|
|   |   |   |   |   |   |   |   |   |   |    |    |    |

Test yourself again and time how long it takes.

**TEST 2**

| 8 × 8 = | | 10 × 8 = | | 4 × 8 = |
|---|---|---|---|---|
| | 7 × 8 = | | 2 × 8 = | |
| 12 × 8 = | | 9 × 8 = | | 0 × 8 = |
| | 6 × 8 = | | 1 × 8 = | |
| 5 × 8 = | | 3 × 8 = | | 11 × 8 = |

**Time taken:**

# Multiplication table for 8

Use your knowledge of the 8 times table to answer these questions.

## WARMING UP

1   How much are eight 5p coins worth? _____

2   How many sides do 4 octagons have? _____

3   Find the product of 6 and 8. _____

4   Multiply 7 by 8. _____

5   Kim saves £8 each month. How much does she save in one year? _____

6   How many legs do 5 octopuses have? _____

7   Multiply (3 × 2) by 8. _____

8   How many eighths are there in 2 wholes? _____

9   There are 11 players in each team. How many players in 8 teams? _____

## GETTING HOTTER

10  Ben gave his six friends 8 stickers each, and he had 12 left over. How many stickers did he have at first? _____

11  Mrs Martin finds a website that sells DVDs at £8 each. She buys 8 DVDs from the site and pays £69 for them including delivery. How much did she pay for delivery? _____

12  In the school hall, 8 children can fit on each bench. How many children can fit on 7 benches? _____

## BURN IT UP!

13  How much greater than 4 × 8 is 8 × 11? _____

14  Is each statement true or false?
   • Multiplying by 8 is the same as multiplying by 4 and then doubling. _____
   • Multiplying by 8 is the same as multiplying by 2 and then doubling and doubling again. _____
   • Multiplying by 8 is the same as doubling, doubling and then doubling again. _____

**How did I do?**

 ☐     ☐     ☐

19

# Division facts for 8

Look at the division facts below, cover them up, then test yourself.

| | |
|---|---|
| 0 ÷ 8 = 0 | |
| 8 ÷ 8 = 1 | |
| 16 ÷ 8 = 2 | |
| 24 ÷ 8 = 3 | |
| 32 ÷ 8 = 4 | |
| 40 ÷ 8 = 5 | |
| 48 ÷ 8 = 6 | |
| 56 ÷ 8 = 7 | |
| 64 ÷ 8 = 8 | |
| 72 ÷ 8 = 9 | |
| 80 ÷ 8 = 10 | |
| 88 ÷ 8 = 11 | |
| 96 ÷ 8 = 12 | |

**TEST 1**

| |
|---|
| 0 ÷ 8 = |
| 8 ÷ 8 = |
| 16 ÷ 8 = |
| 24 ÷ 8 = |
| 32 ÷ 8 = |
| 40 ÷ 8 = |
| 48 ÷ 8 = |
| 56 ÷ 8 = |
| 64 ÷ 8 = |
| 72 ÷ 8 = |
| 80 ÷ 8 = |
| 88 ÷ 8 = |
| 96 ÷ 8 = |

Divide each number by 8. Time yourself.

**TEST 2**

56      24      80      48

............      ............      ............      ............

72      32      0      88      8

............      ............      ............      ............

64      40      16      96

............      ............      ............      ............

**Time taken:**

# Division facts for 8

Use the division facts for 8 to help you answer these questions.

WARMING UP

**1** Divide 88 by 8. _____

**2** How many eights make 80? _____

**3** How many 8 g weights make 64 g? _____

**4** Mel has 8 times as much money as Ed. Mel has £72. How much does Ed have? _____

**5** Share 24 sweets between 8. _____

**6** What is one-eighth of 48? _____

**7** When 56 is divided by 8, what is the answer? _____

**8** How long will it take to travel a distance of 40 km going at 8 km/h? _____

**9** A number multiplied by 8 is 96. What is the number? _____

GETTING HOTTER

**10** An octagon has a perimeter of 80 cm. If all its sides are the same length, what is the length of each side? _____

**11** At a hockey tournament, 88 players get into 8 equal teams. How many players are on each team? _____

**12** How much change is left from £50 if Daniel buys as many £8 pizzas as he can? _____

BURN IT UP!

**13** How many times larger is 72 ÷ 8 than 24 ÷ 8? _____

**14** Rashid's grandma is eight times older than Rashid. If his grandma is 77 years older than Rashid, can you work out how old Rashid is? _____

**How did I do?**

 ☐   ☐   ☐

# Mixed multiplication practice (3 and 4)

The purple rods are 3 cubes long and the green rods are 4 cubes long. Write a multiplication fact for each row of rods. Two have been done for you.

4 × 3 = 12

5 × 4 = 20

..................................

..................................

..................................

..................................

..................................

..................................

..................................

..................................

Complete these multiplications. Time yourself.

| | | |
|---|---|---|
| 4 × 4 = | 3 × 3 = | 7 × 3 = |
| 5 × 3 = | 12 × 4 = | 8 × 3 = |
| 11 × 3 = | 9 × 4 = | 8 × 4 = |
| 0 × 3 = | 12 × 4 = | 9 × 3 = |
| 12 × 3 = | 6 × 4 = | 10 × 3 = |

**Time taken:**

# Mixed multiplication practice (3 and 4)

Use your knowledge of the 3 and 4 times tables to answer these questions.

## WARMING UP

1   What do four 4 g weights and three 3 g weights weigh altogether? ........................

2   Which have more sides – five squares or six triangles? ........................

3   What is the total of 7 × 3 and 6 × 4? ........................

4   What is 3 × 3 × 3? ........................

5   How many 3 g weights weigh the same as six 4 g weights? ........................

6   Find the difference between 8 × 4 and 9 × 3. ........................

7   Multiply zero by three. ........................

8   What is (6 × 4) – (4 × 3)? ........................

## GETTING HOTTER

9   One-third of a mystery number is 12. What is the mystery number?

........................

10  There are seven teams of four players, and two players left over.
    How many players are there in total? ........................

11  At a school fête, calendars are sold for £4 each and diaries for £3 each.
    How much did the school get if it sold 12 calendars and 4 diaries?

........................

## BURN IT UP!

12  A hexagon has sides that are 3 cm long. A square has sides that are 4 cm
    long. Which shape has the longer perimeter and by how much?

13  Answer each question:

    1 × 3 × 3 × 1  ........................          1 × 2 × 3 × 4  ........................

    3 × 4 × 4  ........................          3 × 3 × 4 × 4 × 4 × 0  ........................

**How did I do?**

# Mixed multiplication practice (6 and 8)

The blue rods are 6 cubes long and the yellow rods are 8 cubes long. Write a multiplication fact for each row of rods. Two have been done for you.

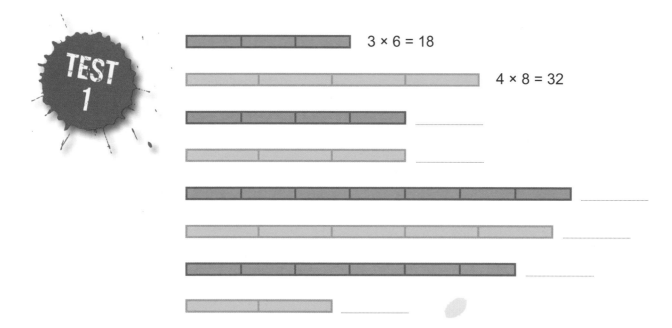

3 × 6 = 18

4 × 8 = 32

Answer these multiplications. Time yourself.

| | | |
|---|---|---|
| 4 × 8 = | 3 × 6 = | 7 × 8 = |
| 3 × 8 = | 12 × 6 = | 8 × 8 = |
| 11 × 6 = | 9 × 6 = | 10 × 6 = |
| 0 × 8 = | 11 × 8 = | 8 × 6 = |
| 7 × 6 = | 6 × 6 = | 12 × 8 = |

**Time taken:**

# Mixed multiplication practice (6 and 8)

Use your knowledge of the 5 and 6 times tables to answer these questions.

## WARMING UP

1   What is 6 × 2 × 8? ...........................

2   Which has more sides – 3 hexagons or 2 octagons? ...........................

3   Multiply six by eight by one. What is the answer? ...........................

4   Find the difference between 7 × 8 and 7 × 6. ...........................

5   Add the product of 6 and 8 to the product of 2 and 6. ...........................

6   Add 3 × 6 and 9 × 8. ...........................

7   Jo has £7. Kim has six times as much. How much has Kim? ...........................

8   How many eights are the same as 4 sixes? ...........................

## GETTING HOTTER

9   A shop sells T-shirts for £8 each and vest tops for £6 each. If it sells
    7 T-shirts and 9 vest tops in one day, how much money did it get?

    ...........................

10  A box has 8 milk chocolates and 6 dark chocolates. How many
    chocolates are there in 4 boxes? ...........................

## BURN IT UP!

11  Subtract the number of days in 6 weeks from the number of months in
    8 years. ...........................

12  Are the answers to these the same? ...........................
    (6 × 4) + (6 × 8)        (8 × 3) + (8 × 6)

13  A bucket holds 8 litres of water. A bowl holds 6 litres of water. How much
    water is there altogether in 4 full buckets and 3 full bowls? ...........................

**How did I do?**

# Mixed division practice (3 and 4)

Finding one-third, $\frac{1}{3}$, is the same as dividing by 3. Finding one-quarter, $\frac{1}{4}$, is the same as dividing by 4. Write the value of each:

**TEST 1**

One-third of 36 ............................

One-quarter of 44 ............................

$\frac{1}{3}$ of 9 ............................

$\frac{1}{4}$ of 20 ............................

One-third of 12 ............................

$\frac{1}{4}$ of 16 ............................

One-quarter of 32 ............................

$\frac{1}{3}$ of 18 ............................

One-third of 30 ............................

$\frac{1}{4}$ of 24 ............................

$\frac{1}{3}$ of 21 ............................

One-third of 27 ............................

One-quarter of 28 ............................

$\frac{1}{4}$ of 36 ............................

One-third of 24 ............................

Answer these questions as quickly as you can. Time yourself.

**TEST 2**

| | |
|---|---|
| $8 \div 4 =$ | $9 \div 3 =$ |
| $3 \div 3 =$ | $36 \div 4 =$ |
| $16 \div 4 =$ | $27 \div 3 =$ |
| $15 \div 3 =$ | $32 \div 4 =$ |
| $12 \div 4 =$ | $21 \div 3 =$ |
| $12 \div 3 =$ | $44 \div 4 =$ |
| $28 \div 4 =$ | $24 \div 3 =$ |
| $0 \div 3 =$ | $48 \div 4 =$ |
| $40 \div 4 =$ | $36 \div 3 =$ |
| $18 \div 3 =$ | $20 \div 4 =$ |
| $4 \div 4 =$ | $33 \div 3 =$ |
| $6 \div 3 =$ | $0 \div 4 =$ |
| $24 \div 4 =$ | $30 \div 3 =$ |

**Time taken:**

# Mixed division practice (3 and 4)

Use your knowledge of the division facts from the 3 and 4 times tables to help you solve these.

## WARMING UP

1  How many £4 magazines cost £32? .................................

2  Divide 48 by 4 and divide the answer by 3. What do you get? .................

3  How many fours are the same as 12 threes? .......................

4  How many threes are the same as 6 fours? ......................

5  Divide 36 by 4 and share the answer between 3. ...................

6  Find the difference between 44 ÷ 4 and 18 ÷ 3. ..................

7  What is the remainder when 29 is divided by 3? ..................

8  What is zero divided by four? .......................

## GETTING HOTTER

9  Some peaches are cut into quarters. If there are 32 quarters, how many whole peaches were there? .....................

10 Potatoes can be bought in 3 kg bags. Each bag costs £4. A fish and chip shop pays £24 for some of these bags. How many kilograms of potatoes did the shop buy? ..................

11 How many 4-litre oil cans can be filled from 28 litres of oil? .................

## BURN IT UP!

12 If four cups of coffee cost £8, how much do three cups of coffee cost?
.........................

13 Squaring a number means multiplying it by itself. What number squared gives the answer 16? ...................

**How did I do?**

 ☐   ☐   ☐

# Mixed division practice (6 and 8)

Finding one-sixth, $\frac{1}{6}$, is the same as dividing by 6. Finding one-eighth, $\frac{1}{8}$, is the same as dividing by 8. Write the value of each:

One-sixth of 42 ................................    One-eighth of 56 ................................

$\frac{1}{6}$ of 54 ................................    $\frac{1}{8}$ of 64 ................................

One-sixth of 18 ................................    $\frac{1}{8}$ of 40 ................................

One-eighth of 72 ................................    $\frac{1}{6}$ of 48 ................................

$\frac{1}{6}$ of 72 ................................    One-eighth of 88 ................................

One-sixth of 36 ................................    $\frac{1}{8}$ of 96 ................................

One-eighth of 48 ................................    $\frac{1}{6}$ of 24 ................................

One-sixth of 66 ................................

Answer these questions as quickly as you can. Time yourself.

| | |
|---|---|
| 12 ÷ 6 = | 80 ÷ 8 = |
| 40 ÷ 8 = | 36 ÷ 6 = |
| 42 ÷ 6 = | 24 ÷ 8 = |
| 8 ÷ 8 = | 24 ÷ 6 = |
| 6 ÷ 6 = | 72 ÷ 8 = |
| 96 ÷ 8 = | 0 ÷ 6 = |
| 66 ÷ 6 = | 32 ÷ 8 = |
| 56 ÷ 8 = | 30 ÷ 6 = |
| 72 ÷ 6 = | 64 ÷ 8 = |
| 16 ÷ 8 = | 60 ÷ 6 = |
| 18 ÷ 6 = | 0 ÷ 8 = |
| 48 ÷ 8 = | 54 ÷ 6 = |
| 48 ÷ 6 = | 88 ÷ 8 = |

**Time taken:**

# Mixed division practice (6 and 8)

Can you solve these problems using the division facts you know?

WARMING UP

1 Add (80 ÷ 8) to (48 ÷ 6). ........................

2 How many less than one-sixth of 42 is one-eighth of 48? ........................

3 How many 8p sweets can I buy with 70p? ........................

4 How many eights are the same as 4 sixes? ........................

5 Divide 48 by 8 and divide the answer by 6. What do you get? ........................

6 How many £8 T-shirts cost £56? ........................

7 Share 96 between 8 and divide the answer by 6. ........................

8 What is the remainder when 55 is divided by 6? ........................

GETTING HOTTER

9 A mobile phone contract charges 6p per minute plus 8p per call. Jo paid 70p for making two calls. For how many minutes in total did the two calls last? ........................

10 In the UK, there are silver coins (5p, 10p, 20p and 50p) and copper coins (1p and 2p). Jack has 6 silver coins and 8 copper coins. The total value of the coins he has is 46p. What coins does he have? ........................

BURN IT UP!

11 The equals sign shows that what is on one side is equal to what is on the other side. For example: 4 × 6 = 3 × 8 ; 40 ÷ 8 = 30 ÷ 6.

Fill in the missing numbers so that each statement is true.

24 ÷ [    ] = 32 ÷ 8          [    ] ÷ 8 = 66 ÷ 6

[    ] ÷ 8 = 42 ÷ 6          8 ÷ [    ] = 6 ÷ 6

48 ÷ 8 = [    ] ÷ 6          96 ÷ 8 = [    ] ÷ 6

**How did I do?**

Each strip of stamps contains 3p, 4p, 6p or 8p stamps. How much is each strip worth?

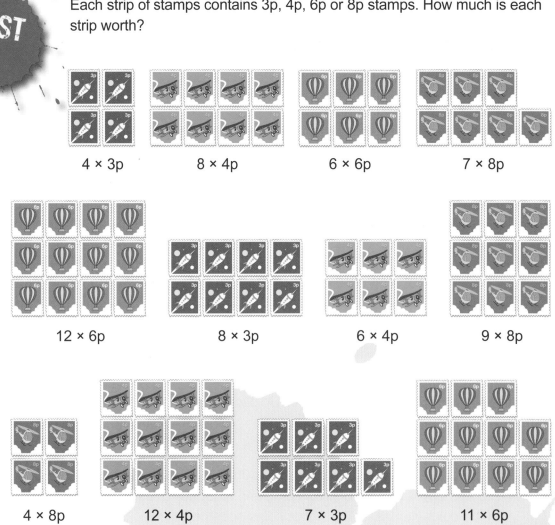

4 × 3p          8 × 4p          6 × 6p          7 × 8p

12 × 6p          8 × 3p          6 × 4p          9 × 8p

4 × 8p          12 × 4p          7 × 3p          11 × 6p

Multiply the number at the left of each row by the number at the top of each column to complete the table. Time yourself.

| × | 5 | 6 | 7 | 9 | 12 |
|---|---|---|---|---|---|
| 3 | 15 | | | | |
| 4 | | | 28 | | |
| 6 | | | | | |
| 8 | | 48 | | | |

**Time taken:**

30

# Mixed multiplication practice (3, 4, 6 and 8)

Use your knowledge of these times tables to answer these questions.

## WARMING UP

1  How many threes are equal to 4 sixes? ........................

2  Subtract 8 × 4 from 7 × 6. ........................

3  Find the product of 5 and 8. ........................

4  Find 3 × 4 and multiply the answer by 6. ........................

5  Find the difference between 4 × 12 and 3 × 6. ........................

6  Find the total of six 6 g weights, three 4 g weights and four 8 g weights.

........................

7  Add 7 × 6, 6 × 4 and 8 × 3. ........................

8  What are 8 groups of 8 plus 9 groups of 4? ........................

9  How much does it cost to buy eight 6p sweets and nine 8p sweets?

........................

## GETTING HOTTER

10  Billy and Milly have the same amount of money. Billy has eight £5 notes and six £1 coins. Milly has four £10 notes and some £2 coins. How many £2 coins does she have? ........................

11  A set of balance scales has six 8 g weights in one pan. How many 4 g weights need to be put in the other pan for the scale to balance?

........................

## BURN IT UP!

12  I'm thinking of a secret number. I multiply it by 8. I also multiply it by 6. When I add the two answers I get 56. What is my secret number?

........................

13  Find the total of:  7 × 3,  5 × 4,  7 × 6  and  9 × 8. ........................

**How did I do?**    ☐    ☐    ☐

# Mixed division practice (3, 4, 6 and 8)

For each number of players, use division to show how many different-sized teams there would be.

**48 players**

in teams of 8

in teams of 6

in teams of 4

**12 players**

in teams of 3

in teams of 6

in teams of 4

**24 players**

in teams of 8

in teams of 6

in teams of 3

**36 players**

in teams of 3

in teams of 6

in teams of 4

Now write how many would be left out if the children got into these different teams. Time yourself.

**43 players**

in teams of 8

in teams of 6

in teams of 4

**29 players**

in teams of 3

in teams of 4

in teams of 6

**37 players**

in teams of 3

in teams of 6

in teams of 8

**23 players**

in teams of 8

in teams of 3

in teams of 4

**Time taken:**

# Mixed division practice (3, 4, 6 and 8)

Use division facts to help you solve these.

## WARMING UP

1  Divide 54 by 6 and the answer by 3. What number do you get? _____

2  How many groups of 6 in 66? _____

3  One-eighth of 64 is one-quarter of what number? _____

4  Add one-sixth of 24 to one-third of 36. _____

5  Add (96 ÷ 8) to (42 ÷ 6). _____

6  How many fours are the same as six eights? _____

7  Find $\frac{1}{4}$ of 32 and multiply the answer by 3. _____

8  Find the difference between 18 ÷ 3 and 32 ÷ 8. _____

9  What is zero divided by eight? _____

## GETTING HOTTER

10  Each of the 10 pods of a Ferris wheel can hold 8 people. There are 60 people on the wheel. 6 pods are full. The other 4 pods have an equal number of people in them. How many people are in each of these 4 pods? _____

11  Lia's father is 4 times older than she is. Her grandma is 8 times older than she is. If Lia's grandma is 56, how old is Lia's father? _____

## BURN IT UP!

12  I'm thinking of a secret number between 30 and 50. When it is divided by 6, the remainder is 4. When it is divided by 8, the remainder is 6. What is the remainder when it is divided by 4? _____

13  Henry buys some stamps at a post office. If he spent 24p on 4p stamps, 66p on 6p stamps and 32p on 8p stamps, how many stamps did he buy altogether? _____

**How did I do?**

 ☐    ☐    ☐

# Problem solving (3 and 4 times tables)

Fill in the missing numbers in these multiplications. Time yourself.

**TEST 1**

4 × 4 = [    ]          [    ] × 3 = 18          4 × [    ] = 20

3 × [    ] = 27          4 × [    ] = 32          [    ] × 4 = 0

3 × 3 = [    ]          [    ] × 4 = 36          4 × [    ] = 44

[    ] × 4 = 48          10 × 4 = [    ]          [    ] × 3 = 36

3 × [    ] = 24          7 × [    ] = 28          11 × 3 = [    ]

This is a magic square. The three numbers in each row, column and diagonal add up to 15. Multiply each number in the square by 4 to create a new set of numbers. Time yourself.

**TEST 2**

| 6 | 7 | 2 |
|---|---|---|
| 1 | 5 | 9 |
| 8 | 3 | 4 |

| 24 | | |
|---|---|---|
| | | |
| | | |

Is the new square a magic square? If so, what do the numbers add up to? ........................

**Time taken:**

# Problem solving (3 and 4 times tables)

## WARMING UP

**1** Add the sixth multiple of 4 to the ninth multiple of 3. ...........................

**2** Is it true that every multiple of 4 is also a multiple of 2? ...........................

**3** Write 3 pairs of facts from the 3 and 4 times tables that have the same answers. ...........................................................................................................................

...........................................................................................................................

## GETTING HOTTER

**4** There are 3p stamps and 4p stamps. Which totals up to 20p can be made with these stamps?

For example: **3p** = 1 × 3p, **4p** = 1 × 4p, **6p** = 2 × 3p, **7p** = 1 × 3p + 1 × 4p.

...........................................................................................................................

...........................................................................................................................

Which totals cannot be made? ...........................................................................

## BURN IT UP!

**5** Write the unit digit of each multiple of 3, from 3 to 36. Do you notice anything about the digits? ...........................................................................

...........................................................................................................................

**6** Write the unit digit of each multiple of 4, from 4 to 48. What do you notice about the digits? ...........................................................................

...........................................................................................................................

**7** Multiply adjacent blue numbers and write them in the spaces in between. (One has been done for you.) Find the total of the four answers. Which of these baubles has the highest total?

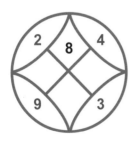 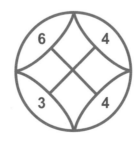 

**How did I do?**

 ☐  ☐  ☐

35

# Problem solving (3 and 4 division facts)

Write a division fact for the 4 times table that gives each number on the clock.

Fill in the missing numbers in these divisions. Time yourself.

4 ÷ 4 = [    ]          [    ] ÷ 3 = 9          24 ÷ [    ] = 8

[    ] ÷ 3 = 3          [    ] ÷ 4 = 7          [    ] ÷ 3 = 0

21 ÷ 3 = [    ]          [    ] ÷ 4 = 9          33 ÷ [    ] = 3

[    ] ÷ 4 = 4          32 ÷ 4 = [    ]          [    ] ÷ 3 = 12

44 ÷ [    ] = 11          24 ÷ [    ] = 6          [    ] ÷ 4 = 12

**Time taken:**

# Problem solving (3 and 4 division facts)

WARMING UP

**1** Write a word problem for each of these divisions:

$18 ÷ 3 = ?$

$0 ÷ 4 = ?$

$48 ÷ 4 = ?$

GETTING HOTTER

**2** Use these digit cards to make as many different division facts as you can. Use each card as many times as you like, for example: $3 ÷ 3 = 1$, $12 ÷ 4 = 3$. Can you make more than 8 division facts from the 3 and 4 times tables?

| 0 | 1 | 2 | 3 | 4 | ÷ | = |
|---|---|---|---|---|---|---|

BURN IT UP!

**3** This is a magic square. Arrange the remaining tiles into the grid so that the three answers in each row, column and diagonal add up to 15.

| $8 ÷ 4$ | $36 ÷ 4$ | $16 ÷ 4$ |
|---|---|---|
|  |  | $12 ÷ 4$ |
|  | $4 ÷ 4$ |  |

$2 + 9 + 4 = 15$

| $32 ÷ 4$ |
|---|

| $28 ÷ 4$ | $20 ÷ 4$ | $24 ÷ 4$ |
|---|---|---|

**How did I do?**

 ☐    ☐    ☐

# Problem solving (6 and 8 times tables)

Fill in the missing numbers in these multiplications. Time yourself.

**TEST 1**

11 × 8 = [    ]          8 × 6 = [    ]          6 × [    ] = 42

8 × [    ] = 80          4 × [    ] = 44          [    ] × 8 = 0

3 × 6 = [    ]          [    ] × 6 = 36          8 × [    ] = 40

[    ] × 8 = 8          9 × 6 = [    ]          [    ] × 8 = 24

8 × [    ] = 72          6 × [    ] = 72          8 × 8 = [    ]

This is a magic square. The three numbers in each row, column and diagonal add up to 15. Multiply each number in the square by 6 to create a new set of numbers. Time yourself.

**TEST 2**

| 4 | 9 | 2 |
|---|---|---|
| 3 | 5 | 7 |
| 8 | 1 | 6 |

| 24 | | |
|---|---|---|
| | | |
| | | |

Is the new square a magic square? If so, what do the numbers add up to? ..................

**Time taken:**

# Problem solving (6 and 8 times tables)

## WARMING UP

**1** Add the eighth multiple of 6 to the ninth multiple of 8. ........................................

**2** Write 3 pairs of tables facts for the 6 and 8 times tables that have the same answers.

## GETTING HOTTER

**3** There are 6p stamps and 8p stamps. Which totals up to 40p can be made with these stamps?
For example: **6p** = 1 × 6p, **8p** = 1 × 8p, **12p** = 2 × 6p, **14p** = 1 × 6p + 1 × 8p.

.......................................................................................................................

.......................................................................................................................

Which totals cannot be made? ...........................................................................

**4** Complete this puzzle using the clues. Write multiplications for the missing clues.

**Across**
- **1** 8 × 8
- **2** 2 × 8
- **3** 8 × 6
- **4** 4 × 8
- **6** ........................
- **7** 6 × 6
- **8** 10 × 8

**Down**
- **1** 11 × 6
- **2** 3 × 6
- **3** 7 × 6
- **4** 6 × 6
- **5** 12 × 8
- **6** 9 × 6
- **7** ........................

|   |   |   |   |   |   |
|---|---|---|---|---|---|
| 1 |   | ▓ | 2 |   |   |
|   | ▓ | 3 |   |   | ▓ |
| ▓ | 4 |   |   | ▓ | 5 |
| 6 |   | ▓ |   | 7 |   |
|   | ▓ | 8 |   |   | ▓ |

## BURN IT UP!

**5** Follow these rules and look for a pattern.

> Choose a **multiple of 4** between 1 and 15.
> Multiply the number by 6, then divide the answer by 8.

What is special about all of the answers? ...............................................

**How did I do?**

# Problem solving (6 and 8 division facts)

Write a division fact for the 8 times table that gives each number on the clock.

**TEST 1**

Fill in the missing numbers in these divisions. Time yourself.

**TEST 2**

42 ÷ 6 = [      ]          [      ] ÷ 8 = 9          80 ÷ [      ] = 8

18 ÷ [      ] = 3          36 ÷ [      ] = 6          [      ] ÷ 6 = 0

56 ÷ 8 = [      ]          [      ] ÷ 6 = 9          [      ] ÷ 8 = 3

[      ] ÷ 6 = 4          48 ÷ 6 = [      ]          [      ] ÷ 8 = 12

66 ÷ [      ] = 11          64 ÷ [      ] = 8          [      ] ÷ 6 = 12

**Time taken:**

# Problem solving (6 and 8 division facts)

1   Write two multiplication and two division statements that each use the numbers 8, 6 and 48. ........................................................

2   Is it true that every number that is divisible by 6 is also divisible by 3?

    ........................................................

3   Place numbers between 20 and 75 into this diagram.

   Numbers divisible by 6     Numbers divisible by 8

   What do you notice about the numbers in the section in the middle?

   ........................................................

   ........................................................

4   This is a magic square. Arrange the remaining tiles into the grid so that the three answers in each row, column and diagonal make a total of 15.

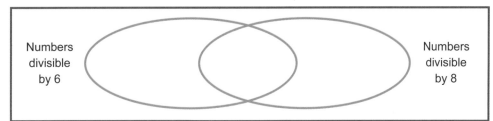

| 12 ÷ 6 | 56 ÷ 8 | 48 ÷ 8 |
|--------|--------|--------|
|        |        |        |
|        | 18 ÷ 6 |        |

2 + 7 + 6 = 15

8 ÷ 8

72 ÷ 8

30 ÷ 6

24 ÷ 6    64 ÷ 8

**How did I do?**

Fill in the missing numbers so that every joined question has the same answer.

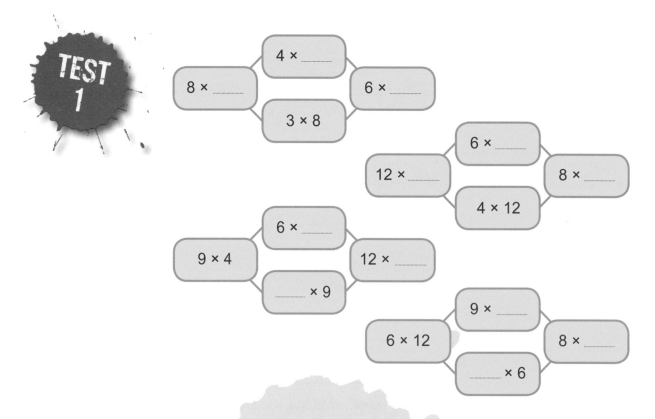

Fill in the missing numbers in these divisions. Time yourself.

9 × 3 = [    ]          [    ] × 4 = 44          6 × [    ] = 48

8 × [    ] = 96          6 × [    ] = 42          [    ] × 3 = 0

7 × 4 = [    ]          [    ] × 6 = 36          8 × [    ] = 56

[    ] × 3 = 3          9 × 4 = [    ]          [    ] × 3 = 27

8 × [    ] = 88          6 × [    ] = 54          12 × 6 = [    ]

Time taken:

# Problem solving (3, 4, 6 and 8 times tables)

## WARMING UP

**1** Answer these questions:

$6 × 2 × 6 =$ ........    $3 × 3 × 6 =$ ........    $3 × 4 × 8 =$ ........    $4 × 8 × 6 × 0 =$ ........

**2** What is the ninth multiple of 4 plus the seventh multiple of 6? ........................

## GETTING HOTTER

**3** Fill in the missing digits to make each answer correct.

Can you complete the second grid in the same way?

Make up more of your own puzzles.

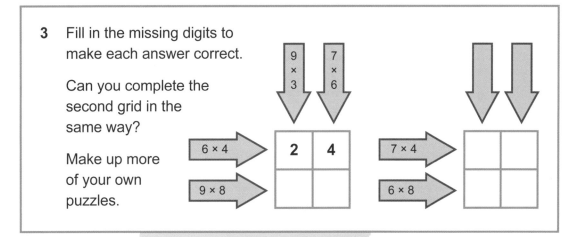

## BURN IT UP!

**4** Use these digit cards to make as many different tables facts as you can. You can use each card as many times as you like, for example: $6 × 8 = 48$, $2 × 6 = 12$. Can you make more than 20 different facts from your 3, 4, 6 and 8 times tables?

| 1 | 2 | 3 | 4 | 6 | 8 | × | = |

........................................................................

........................................................................

........................................................................

**How did I do?**

 ☐    ☐    ☐

# Problem solving (3, 4, 6 and 8 division facts)

Find sets of questions with the same answer. Colour each set the same colour.

| | | | | |
|---|---|---|---|---|
| 96 ÷ 8 | 0 ÷ 8 | 30 ÷ 3 | 42 ÷ 6 | 12 ÷ 4 |
| 36 ÷ 6 | 12 ÷ 2 | 18 ÷ 6 | 40 ÷ 4 | 80 ÷ 8 |
| 36 ÷ 3 | 48 ÷ 6 | 36 ÷ 4 | 6 ÷ 6 | 0 ÷ 4 |
| 40 ÷ 8 | 3 ÷ 3 | 30 ÷ 6 | 27 ÷ 3 | 72 ÷ 8 |
| 72 ÷ 6 | 64 ÷ 8 | 42 ÷ 6 | 33 ÷ 3 | 60 ÷ 6 |
| 8 ÷ 4 | 24 ÷ 8 | 66 ÷ 6 | 28 ÷ 4 | 16 ÷ 8 |

Fill in the missing numbers in these divisions. Time yourself.

48 ÷ 4 = [   ]     [   ] ÷ 8 = 7     48 ÷ [   ] = 8

36 ÷ 6 = [   ]     [   ] ÷ 4 = 8     [   ] ÷ 6 = 0

[   ] ÷ 6 = 7     64 ÷ 8 = [   ]     [   ] ÷ 6 = 12

54 ÷ [   ] = 9     96 ÷ [   ] = 12     [   ] ÷ 3 = 9

**Time taken:**

# Problem solving (3, 4, 6 and 8 division facts)

## WARMING UP

**1** Kim spent £1.20 on 4p, 6p and 8p stamps. She bought twice as many 6p stamps as 4p stamps. If she bought nine 8p stamps, what other stamps did she buy? _____

**2** Find the total of the ninth multiple of 4, the fourth multiple of 6, the second multiple of 3 and the seventh multiple of 8.

## GETTING HOTTER

**3** Use these digit cards to make as many different division facts as you can. You can use each card as many times as you like, for example: 18 ÷ 3 = 6, 48 ÷ 4 = 12. Can you make more than 20 different division facts related to the 3, 4, 6 and 8 times tables?

| 1 | 2 | 3 | 4 | 6 | 8 | ÷ | = |

## BURN IT UP!

**4** Use the clues to fill in this puzzle. Write divisions or multiplications for the missing clues.

**Across**
- **1** 44 ÷ 4
- **2** 36 ÷ 3
- **3** 5 × 8
- **4** 72 ÷ 6
- **6** _____
- **7** 48 ÷ 4
- **8** 8 × 6

**Down**
- **1** 96 ÷ 8
- **2** 60 ÷ 6
- **3** 7 × 6
- **4** 88 ÷ 8
- **5** 9 × 8
- **6** 3 × 8
- **7** _____

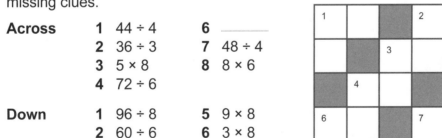

**How did I do?**

# Hints and tips

When learning your times tables and related division facts there are some useful things to remember:

- The order of the numbers in a multiplication question doesn't matter as the answer will be the same, for example $6 \times 2 = 12$ and $2 \times 6 = 12$. It means that you learn two facts for the price of one!

- If you know multiplication facts then you also know related division facts. If you know that $6 \times 2 = 12$ and $2 \times 6 = 12$ then you also know that $12 \div 2 = 6$ and $12 \div 6 = 2$. This means that you actually learn four facts for the price of one!

- You might find it easier to learn the facts in order at first, but make sure that you begin to learn to answer questions in any order.

- Look for patterns in the numbers to help you check your answers. For example: the answers for the facts in the 2, 4, 6 and 8 times tables are always even; the answers to the 10 times table end in 0; the answers to the 5 times table end in 0 or 5; the digits of the answers to the 9 times table always add up to 9 or 18 and so on.

- As you learn a table there will always be some facts that you find more difficult to remember than others. Focus on learning these facts using the tips below.

Try these different approaches:

- Say facts aloud using a range of voices: high or low voices, whispering, croaking, singing, shouting, speaking with the voice of a cat, snake, worm, monster and so on.

- Write questions onto small pieces of paper or card and the answers on the other side. Use them to test yourself at different times. Put them on the fridge, on a noticeboard or even on your stairs. Each time you see the card try to remember the answer.

- Draw pictures for the questions you find most difficult, such as drawing a picture of 5 rows of 9 flowers to help you with the question 'How many 5s in 45?'

- Write out facts in words rather than just using numbers, such as for $24 \div 2$ writing 'twenty-four divided by two is twelve'.

- Make up rhymes and songs to help you learn facts that you find difficult to remember, such as 'Clap, bang, thump the floor because 8 times 8 is sixty-four' or 'Turn off the telly and touch the screen as 4 lots of 4 equals sixteen'. Use movements and gestures in the rhymes as this can also help you to remember them more easily.

# Answers

## Multiplication table for 3 (pages 6–7)

**Test 1** 9, 15, 3, 30, 12, 18, 21, 24, 27, 6, 33, 36

**Test 2** 33, 24, 12, 21
3, 9, 27, 0
36, 30, 0, 18
6, 18, 27, 15

| | | | | | |
|---|---|---|---|---|---|
| **1** | 18 | **2** | 27 | **3** | 36 |
| **4** | 21 | **5** | 9 | **6** | 33 |
| **7** | 12 | **8** | 0 | **9** | £24 |
| **10** | £6 | **11** | 18 | **12** | 24 cm |
| **13** | 12 | **14** | 36 cm | | |

## Division facts for 3 (pages 8–9)

**Test 1** 0, 1, 2, 3, 4, 5, 6, 7, 8, 9, 10, 11, 12

**Test 2** 8, 11, 4, 3, 5
7, 10, 12, 9, 6

| | | | | | |
|---|---|---|---|---|---|
| **1** | 5 | **2** | 2 | **3** | 3 |
| **4** | 4 | **5** | 12 | **6** | 10 |
| **7** | 0 | **8** | 1 | **9** | 6 |
| **10** | 9 | **11** | 11 cm | **12** | 3 |

**13** False – it is only true if the even number is a multiple of 3.

**14** True

## Multiplication table for 4 (pages 10–11)

**Test 1**

| | | |
|---|---|---|
| 0 × 4 | double 2 and double again | 8 |
| 1 × 4 | double 1 and double again | 12 |
| 2 × 4 | double 0 and double again | 0 |
| 3 × 4 | double 5 and double again | 16 |
| 4 × 4 | double 4 and double again | 20 |
| 5 × 4 | double 3 and double again | 4 |
| 6 × 4 | double 7 and double again | 44 |
| 7 × 4 | double 6 and double again | 28 |
| 8 × 4 | double 10 and double again | 24 |
| 9 × 4 | double 9 and double again | 48 |
| 10 × 4 | double 8 and double again | 32 |
| 11 × 4 | double 12 and double again | 40 |
| 12 × 4 | double 11 and double again | 36 |

**Test 2** 0, 24, 16, 40, 28
36, 48, 32, 48, 12, 8
36, 4, 0, 44, 20

| | | | | | |
|---|---|---|---|---|---|
| **1** | 40p | **2** | 8 | **3** | 24 |
| **4** | 48 | **5** | 32 | **6** | 36 kg |
| **7** | 28 | **8** | 44 | **9** | 48 |
| **10** | 32 | **11** | £28 | **12** | 44 |
| **13** | 32 | **14** | 20 | **15** | 10 |

## Division facts for 4 (pages 12–13)

**Test 1**

| | | |
|---|---|---|
| 0 ÷ 4 | halve 8 and halve again | 0 |
| 4 ÷ 4 | halve 4 and halve again | 1 |
| 8 ÷ 4 | halve 0 and halve again | 4 |
| 12 ÷ 4 | halve 12 and halve again | 3 |
| 16 ÷ 4 | halve 20 and halve again | 5 |
| 20 ÷ 4 | halve 16 and halve again | 2 |
| 24 ÷ 4 | halve 28 and halve again | 8 |
| 28 ÷ 4 | halve 32 and halve again | 6 |
| 32 ÷ 4 | halve 24 and halve again | 7 |
| 36 ÷ 4 | halve 48 and halve again | 10 |
| 40 ÷ 4 | halve 40 and halve again | 9 |
| 44 ÷ 4 | halve 44 and halve again | 12 |
| 48 ÷ 4 | halve 36 and halve again | 11 |

## Multiplication table for 6 (pages 14–15)

**Test 1** 0, 6, 12, 18, 24, 30, 36, 42, 48, 54, 60, 66, 72

**Test 2** 72, 12, 60, 18
54, 30, 42, 24, 66
48, 36, 6, 0

| | | | | | |
|---|---|---|---|---|---|
| **1** | 30p | **2** | 24 | **3** | 36 |
| **4** | £48 | **5** | 54 g | **6** | 66 |
| **7** | 0 | **8** | 72 | **9** | 60 |
| **10** | 18 | **11** | £3 | **12** | 12 km |
| **13** | 40p | **14** | 42 | **15** | 12 cm |

## Division facts for 6 (pages 16–17)

**Test 1**

$12 ÷ 6 = 2,\quad 18 ÷ 6 = 3,\quad 24 ÷ 6 = 4,$
$30 ÷ 6 = 5,\quad 36 ÷ 6 = 6,\quad 42 ÷ 6 = 7,$
$48 ÷ 6 = 8,\quad 54 ÷ 6 = 9,\quad 60 ÷ 6 = 10,$
$66 ÷ 6 = 11,\quad 72 ÷ 6 = 12$

**Test 2** 5, 6, 11, 8
12, 4, 10, 7, 0
1, 2, 9, 3

| | | | | | |
|---|---|---|---|---|---|
| **1** | 6 | **2** | 11 | **3** | 7 |
| **4** | 12 | **5** | 10 | **6** | 9 |
| **7** | 5 | **8** | 8 | **9** | 4 |
| **10** | 8 seconds | **11** | 1 | **12** | 11 |
| **13** | £24 | **14** | 10 | | |

## Multiplication table for 8 (pages 18–19)

**Test 1** 0, 8, 16, 24, 32, 40, 48, 56, 64, 72, 80, 88, 96

**Test 2** 64, 80, 32
56, 16
96, 72, 0
48, 8,
40, 24, 88

| | | | | | |
|---|---|---|---|---|---|
| **1** | 40p | **2** | 32 | **3** | 48 |
| **4** | 56 | **5** | £96 | **6** | 40 |
| **7** | 48 | **8** | 16 | **9** | 88 |
| **10** | 60 | **11** | £5 | **12** | 56 |
| **13** | 56 | **14** | True, true, true | | |

## Division facts for 8 (pages 20–21)

**Test 1** 0, 1, 2, 3, 4, 5, 6, 7, 8, 9, 10, 11, 12

**Test 2** 7, 3, 10, 6
9, 4, 0, 11, 1
8, 5, 2, 12

| | | | | | |
|---|---|---|---|---|---|
| **1** | 11 | **2** | 10 | **3** | 8 |
| **4** | £9 | **5** | 3 | **6** | 6 |
| **7** | 7 | **8** | 5 hours | **9** | 12 |
| **10** | 10 cm | **11** | 11 | **12** | £2 |
| **13** | 3 | **14** | 11 (and Grandma is 88) | | |

## Mixed multiplication practice (3 and 4) (pages 22–23)

**Test 1** $8 × 3 = 24,\quad 9 × 4 = 36,\quad 6 × 3 = 18,$
$7 × 4 = 28,\quad 5 × 3 = 15,\quad 8 × 4 = 32,$
$9 × 3 = 27,\quad 11 × 4 = 44$

**Test 2** 11, 10, 0, 1, 2, 4, 12, 6, 3, 9, 5, 7, 8

| | | | | | |
|---|---|---|---|---|---|
| **1** | 10 | **2** | 8 | **3** | 9 |
| **4** | 7 | **5** | 6 | **6** | 11 |
| **7** | 3 | **8** | 12 | **9** | 6 |
| **10** | 4 | **11** | 4 | **12** | 2 |

**13** 8 litres, costing £32

## Mixed multiplication practice (6 and 8) (pages 24–25)

**Test 2** 16, 9, 21
15, 48, 24
33, 36, 32
0, 48, 27
36, 24, 30

| | | | | | |
|---|---|---|---|---|---|
| **1** | 25 g | **2** | Five squares | **3** | 45 |
| **4** | 27 | **5** | 8 | **6** | 5 |
| **7** | 0 | **8** | 12 | **9** | 36 |
| **10** | 30 | **11** | £60 | | |

**12** The perimeter of the hexagon is 2 cm longer.

**13** 9, 24  48, 0

## Mixed multiplication practice (6 and 8) (pages 24–25)

**Test 1** $4 × 6 = 24,\quad 3 × 8 = 24,\quad 7 × 6 = 42,$
$5 × 8 = 40,\quad 6 × 6 = 36,\quad 2 × 8 = 16,$
$5 × 6 = 30$

**Test 2** 32, 18, 56
24, 72, 64
66, 54, 60
0, 88, 48
42, 36, 96

| | | | | | |
|---|---|---|---|---|---|
| **1** | 96 | **2** | 3 hexagons | **3** | 48 |
| **4** | 14 | **5** | 60 | **6** | 90 |
| **7** | £42 | **8** | 3 | **9** | £110 |
| **10** | 56 | **11** | 54 | **12** | Yes (72) |

**13** 50 litres

## Mixed division practice (3 and 4) (pages 26–27)

**Test 1** 12, 11,
3, 5,
4, 4
8, 6,
10, 6,
7, 9,
7, 9,
8

**Test 2** 2, 1, 4, 5, 3, 4, 7, 0, 10, 6, 1, 2, 6
3, 9, 9, 8, 7, 11, 8, 12, 12, 5, 11, 0, 10

| | | | | | |
|---|---|---|---|---|---|
| **1** | 8 | **2** | 4 | **3** | 9 |
| **4** | 8 | **5** | 3 | **6** | 5 |
| **7** | 2 | **8** | 0 | **9** | 8 |
| **10** | 18 kg | **11** | 7 | | |
| **12** | £6 | **13** | 4 | | |

## Mixed division practice (6 and 8) (pages 28–29)

**Test 1** 7, 7,
9, 8,
3, 5
9, 8,
12, 11,
6, 12
6, 4,
11

**Test 2** 2, 5, 7, 1, 1, 12, 11, 7, 12, 2, 3, 6, 8
10, 6, 3, 4, 9, 0, 4, 5, 8, 10, 0, 9, 11

# Answers

**1** 18  **2** 1  **3** 8 (6p change)
**4** 3  **5** 1  **6** 7
**7** 2  **8** 1  **9** 9 minutes
**10** 6 × 5p coins + 8 × 2p
**11** 6, 88  56, 8  36, 72

## Mixed multiplication practice (3, 4, 6 and 8) (pages 30–31)

**Test 1**  12p, 32p, 36p, 56p = £1.36
72p, 24p, 24p, 72p = £1.92
32p, 48p, 21p, 66p = £1.67

**Test 2**  15, 18, 21, 27, 36
20, 24, 28, 36, 48
30, 36, 42, 54, 72
40, 48, 56, 72, 96

**1** 8  **2** 10  **3** 40
**4** 72  **5** 30  **6** 80 g
**7** 90  **8** 100  **9** £1.20
**10** 3  **11** 12  **12** 4
**13** 155

## Mixed division practice (3, 4, 6 and 8) (pages 32–33)

**Test 1**  6, 8, 12
4, 2, 3
3, 4, 8
12, 6, 9

**Test 2**  3, 1, 3
2, 1, 5
1, 1, 5
7, 2, 3

**1** 3  **2** 11  **3** 32
**4** 16  **5** 19  **6** 12
**7** 24  **8** 2  **9** 0
**10** 3  **11** 28
**12** 2 (the secret number is 46)  **13** 21

## Problem solving (3 and 4 times tables) (pages 34–35)

**Test 1**  16, 6, 5
9, 8, 0
9, 9, 11
12, 40, 12
8, 4, 33

**Test 2**  24, 28, 8
4, 20, 36
32, 12, 16
Yes, totals add up to 60.

**1** 51  **2** Yes
**3** 4 × 3 = 12,  3 × 4 = 12,  8 × 3 = 24,
6 × 4 = 24,  12 × 3 = 36,  9 × 4 = 36
**4** 3p = 1 × 3p,  4p = 1 × 4p,
6p = 2 × 3p,  7p = 1 × 3p + 1 × 4p,
8p = 2 × 4p,  9p = 3 × 3p,
10p = 2 × 3p + 1 × 4p,  11p = 1 × 3p + 2 × 4p,
12p = 4 × 3p or 3 × 4p,  13p = 3 × 3p + 1 × 4p,
14p = 2 × 3p + 2 × 4p,  15p = 1 × 3p + 3 × 4p,
16p = 4 × 4p,  17p = 3 × 3p + 2 × 4p,
18p = 2 × 3p + 3 × 4p,  19p = 1 × 3p + 4 × 4p,
20p = 5 × 4p
5p cannot be made.
**5** 3, 6, 9, 2, 5, 8, 1, 4, 7, 0, 3, 6 … All the digits occur and then the order begins to repeat.
**6** 4, 8, 2, 6, 0, 4, 8, 2, 6, 0, 4, 8 … Only even digits occur and the pattern 4, 8, 2, 6, 0 repeats.
**7** 18 + 8 + 12 + 27 = 65; 18 + 24 + 16 + 12 = 70; 15 + 20 + 28 + 21 = 84.

## Problem solving (3 and 4 division facts) (pages 36–37)

**Test 1**  4 ÷ 4 = 1,  8 ÷ 4 = 2,  12 ÷ 4 = 3,
16 ÷ 4 = 4,  20 ÷ 4 = 5,  24 ÷ 4 = 6,
28 ÷ 4 = 7,  32 ÷ 4 = 8,  36 ÷ 4 = 9,
40 ÷ 4 = 10,  44 ÷ 4 = 11,  48 ÷ 4 = 12

**Test 2**  1, 27, 3
9, 28, 0
7, 36, 11
16, 8, 36
4, 4, 48

**1** Answers will vary
**2** Possible answers include:
0 ÷ 3 = 0,  3 ÷ 3 = 1,  12 ÷ 3 = 4,
30 ÷ 3 = 10,  33 ÷ 3 = 11,  36 ÷ 3 = 12,
0 ÷ 4 = 0,  4 ÷ 4 = 1,  12 ÷ 4 = 3,
40 ÷ 4 = 10,  44 ÷ 4 = 11
**3** Middle: 28 ÷ 4,  20 ÷ 4  Bottom: 24 ÷ 4,  32 ÷ 4

## Problem solving (6 and 8 times tables) (pages 38–39)

**Test 1**  88, 48, 7
10, 11, 0
18, 6, 5
1, 54, 3
9, 12, 64

**Test 2**  24, 54, 12
18, 30, 42
48, 6, 36
Yes, totals add up to 90.

**1** 120
**2** 4 × 6 = 24,  3 × 8 = 24,  8 × 6 = 48,
6 × 8 = 48,  12 × 6 = 72,  9 × 8 = 72
**3** 6p = 1 × 6p,  8p = 1 × 8p,
12p = 2 × 6p,  14p = 1 × 6p + 1 × 8p,
16p = 2 × 8p,  18p = 3 × 6p,
20p = 2 × 6p + 1 × 8p,  22p = 1 × 6p + 2 × 8p,
24p = 4 × 6p or 3 × 8p,  26p = 3 × 6p + 1 × 8p,
28p = 2 × 6p + 2 × 8p,  30p = 1 × 6p + 3 × 8p,
32p = 4 × 8p,  34p = 3 × 6p + 2 × 8p,
36p = 2 × 6p + 3 × 8p,  38p = 1 × 6p + 4 × 8p,
40p = 5 × 8p
Odd numbers cannot be made.
**4** Across: 1. 64; 2. 16; 3. 48; 4. 32; 6. 56; 7. 36; 8. 80  Down: 1. 66; 2. 18; 3. 42; 4. 36; 5. 96; 6. 54; 7. 30
6 across clue: 7 × 8;
7 down clue: 5 × 6
**5** They are multiples of 3.

## Problem solving (6 and 8 division facts) (pages 40–41)

**Test 1**  8 ÷ 8 = 1,  16 ÷ 8 = 2,  24 ÷ 8 = 3,
32 ÷ 8 = 4,  40 ÷ 8 = 5,  48 ÷ 8 = 6,
56 ÷ 8 = 7,  64 ÷ 8 = 8,  72 ÷ 8 = 9,
80 ÷ 8 = 10,  88 ÷ 8 = 11,  96 ÷ 8 = 12

**Test 2**  7, 72, 10
6, 6, 0
7, 54, 24
24, 8, 96
6, 8, 72

**1** 6 × 8 = 48,  8 × 6 = 48,  48 ÷ 6 = 8,  48 ÷ 8 = 6
**2** Yes
**3** 6: 30, 36, 42, 54, 60, 66, 74; 8: 32, 40, 56, 68; middle: 24, 48, 72. The numbers in the overlapping section are multiples of 24.
**4** Middle: 72 ÷ 8, 30 ÷ 6, 8 ÷ 8
Bottom: 24 ÷ 6, 64 ÷ 8

## Problem solving (3, 4, 6 and 8 times tables) (pages 42–43)

**Test 1**  4 × 6,  6 × 4,  8 × 3
6 × 8,  8 × 6,  12 × 4
6 × 6,  12 × 3,  4 × 9
9 × 8,  8 × 9,  12 × 6

**Test 2**  27, 11, 8
12, 7, 0
28, 6, 7
1, 36, 9
11, 9, 72

**1** 72, 54, 96, 0
**2** 78
**3** 1st grid bottom row **72**; 2nd grid top row **28**, bottom row **48**. 1st arrow **8 × 3** and **6 × 4**; 2nd arrow **11 × 8**
**4** There are more than 28 possible solutions.

## Problem solving (3, 4, 6 and 8 division facts) (pages 44–45)

**Test 1**

| 96 ÷ 8 | 0 ÷ 8 | 30 ÷ 3 | 42 ÷ 6 | 12 ÷ 4 |
|---|---|---|---|---|
| 36 ÷ 6 | 12 ÷ 2 | 18 ÷ 6 | 40 ÷ 4 | 80 ÷ 8 |
| 36 ÷ 3 | 48 ÷ 6 | 36 ÷ 4 | 6 ÷ 6 | 0 ÷ 4 |
| 40 ÷ 8 | 3 ÷ 3 | 30 ÷ 6 | 27 ÷ 3 | 72 ÷ 8 |
| 72 ÷ 6 | 64 ÷ 8 | 42 ÷ 6 | 33 ÷ 3 | 60 ÷ 6 |
| 8 ÷ 4 | 24 ÷ 8 | 66 ÷ 6 | 28 ÷ 4 | 16 ÷ 8 |

**Test 2**  12, 56, 6
6, 32, 0
42, 8, 72
6, 8, 27

**1** 3 × 4p, 6 × 6p
**2** 122
**3** There are more than 28 possible solutions.
**4** Across: 1. 11, 2. 12, 3. 40, 4. 12, 6. 21, 7. 12, 8. 48;  Down: 1. 12, 2. 10, 3. 42, 4. 11, 5. 72, 6. 24, 7. 18
6 across clue: 7 × 3; 7 down clue: 6 × 3